# Daily Gratitude Journal

## Start with Gratitude - spend 5 minutes a day to feel happy

Jennifer Clarke

ISBN- 9798561809415

*Gratitude helps you fall in love
with the life you already have.*

List things you have every day and you can be grateful for _____

_____

_____

_____

_____

_____


List people you have in your life and you are thankful for _____

_____

_____

_____

_____

_____

_____


List important / life changing moments in your life that you are grateful for _____

_____

_____

_____

_____

_____

_____


List people you've never met, but they made difference to your life _____

_____

_____

_____

_____

_____

_____

List moments in your life when you felt proud of yourself _____

_____

_____

_____

_____

_____

_____


List negative events that led to positive changes _____

_____

_____

_____

_____

_____

_____


List things that make you smile _____

_____

_____

_____

_____

_____

_____

_____


List things that make you feel alive _____

_____

_____

_____

_____

_____

_____

*It is not happy people who are grateful,*
*It is grateful people who are happy.*

My thoughts _____

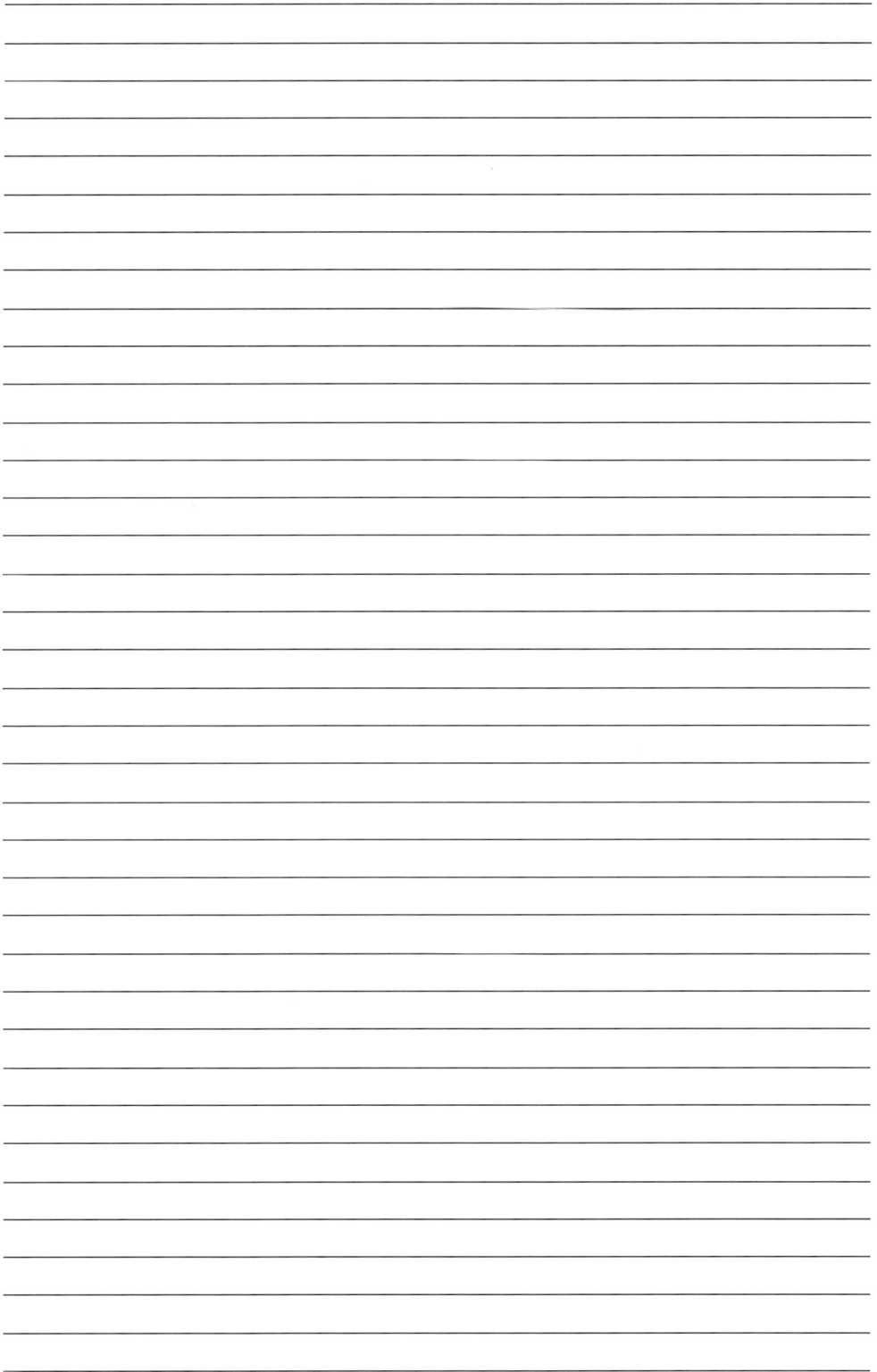

Date _____

Today I am thankful for _____
_____
_____
_____
_____

I am proud of myself because __ _____
_____
_____
_____
_____

My small victory today _____
_____


Date _____

Today I am thankful for _____
_____
_____
_____
_____

The person I am thankful for today is _____
_____
_____

What I did today for myself is _____
_____
_____
_____

Date _____

Today I am thankful for _____
_____
_____
_____
_____

I realized today that _____
_____
_____

I felt happy today when _____
_____
_____
_____

Date _____

Today I am thankful for _____
_____
_____
_____
_____

I felt happy today when _____
_____
_____

What's going on well in my life is _____
_____
_____
_____

Date _____

Today I am thankful for _____

_____

_____

_____

_____

I relized today that _____   _____

_____

_____

_____

I felt happy today when _____

_____

_____

_____

Date _____

Today I am thankful for _____

_____

_____

_____

_____

Good things I noticed today _____

_____

_____

What's going on well in my life is _____

_____

_____

_____

Date _____

Today I am thankful for _____
_____
_____
_____
_____

I am proud of myself because _____
_____
_____
_____
_____

My small victory today _____
_____


Date _____

Today I am thankful for _____
_____
_____
_____
_____

The person I am thankful for today is _____
_____
_____

What I did today for myself is _____
_____
_____
_____

Date _____

Today I am thankful for _____

_____

_____

_____

_____

I realized today that _____

_____

_____

I felt happy today when _____

_____

_____

_____


Date _____

Today I am thankful for _____

_____

_____

_____

_____

I felt happy today when _____

_____

_____

What's going on well in my life is _____

_____

_____

_____

Date _____

Today I am thankful for _____
_____
_____
_____
_____

I relized today that _____
_____
_____
_____

I felt happy today when _____
_____
_____
_____

Date _____

Today I am thankful for _____
_____
_____
_____
_____

Good things I noticed today _____
_____
_____

What's going on well in my life is _____
_____
_____
_____

Date _____

Today I am thankful for _____

_____

_____

_____

_____

I realized today that _____

_____

_____

I felt happy today when _____

_____

_____

_____

Date _____

Today I am thankful for _____

_____

_____

_____

_____

I felt happy today when _____

_____

_____

What's going on well in my life is _____

_____

_____

_____

# Weekly Gratitude

This week I am grateful for _____

_____

_____

_____

_____

_____

_____

_____

_____

_____


5 things I am lucky to have in my life _____

_____

_____

_____

_____

_____

_____

_____

_____


3 people I am lucky to have right now _____

_____

_____

_____

_____

_____

Date _____

Today I am thankful for _____
_____
_____
_____
_____

I am proud of myself because _____
_____
_____
_____
_____

My small victory today _____
_____

Date _____

Today I am thankful for _____
_____
_____
_____
_____

The person I am thankful for today is _____
_____
_____

What I did today for myself is _____
_____
_____
_____

Date _____

Today I am thankful for _____
_____
_____
_____
_____

I realized today that _____
_____
_____

I felt happy today when _____
_____
_____
_____

Date _____

Today I am thankful for _____
_____
_____
_____
_____

I felt happy today when _____
_____
_____

What's going on well in my life is _____
_____
_____
_____

Date _____

Today I am thankful for _____
_____
_____
_____
_____

I relized today that _____
_____
_____
_____

I felt happy today when _____
_____
_____
_____

Date _____

Today I am thankful for _____
_____
_____
_____
_____

Good things I noticed today _____
_____
_____

What's going on well in my life is _____
_____
_____
_____

Date \_\_\_\_\_

Today I am thankful for _____
_____
_____
_____
_____

I am proud of myself because _____
_____
_____
_____
_____

My small victory today _____
_____

Date \_\_\_\_\_

Today I am thankful for _____
_____
_____
_____
_____

The person I am thankful for today is _____
_____
_____

What I did today for myself is _____
_____
_____
_____

Date _____

Today I am thankful for _____

_____

_____

_____

_____

I realized today that _____

_____

_____

I felt happy today when _____

_____

_____

_____


Date _____

Today I am thankful for _____

_____

_____

_____

_____

I felt happy today when _____

_____

_____

What's going on well in my life is _____

_____

_____

_____

Date _____

Today I am thankful for _____
_____
_____
_____
_____
_____

I relized today that _____
_____
_____
_____

I felt happy today when _____
_____
_____
_____

Date _____

Today I am thankful for _____
_____
_____
_____
_____

Good things I noticed today _____
_____
_____

What's going on well in my life is _____
_____
_____
_____

Date \_\_\_\_\_

Today I am thankful for _____

I realized today that _____

I felt happy today when _____

Date \_\_\_\_\_

Today I am thankful for _____

I felt happy today when _____

What's going on well in my life is _____

# Weekly Gratitude

This week I am grateful for _____

_____

_____

_____

_____

_____

_____

_____

_____

5 things I am lucky to have in my life _____

_____

_____

_____

_____

_____

_____

_____

3 people I am lucky to have right now _____

_____

_____

_____

_____

Date _____

Today I am thankful for _____
_____
_____
_____
_____

I am proud of myself because _____
_____
_____
_____
_____

My small victory today _____
_____

Date _____

Today I am thankful for _____
_____
_____
_____
_____

The person I am thankful for today is _____
_____
_____

What I did today for myself is _____
_____
_____
_____

Date _____

Today I am thankful for _____
_____
_____
_____
_____
_____

I realized today that _____
_____
_____

I felt happy today when _____
_____
_____
_____

Date _____

Today I am thankful for _____
_____
_____
_____
_____

I felt happy today when _____
_____
_____

What's going on well in my life is _____
_____
_____
_____

Date _____

Today I am thankful for _____
_____
_____
_____
_____

I relized today that _____
_____
_____
_____

I felt happy today when _____
_____
_____
_____

Date _____

Today I am thankful for _____
_____
_____
_____
_____

Good things I noticed today _____
_____
_____

What's going on well in my life is _____
_____
_____
_____

Date _____

Today I am thankful for _____
_____
_____
_____
_____

I am proud of myself because _____
_____
_____
_____
_____

My small victory today _____
_____

Date _____

Today I am thankful for _____
_____
_____
_____
_____

The person I am thankful for today is _____
_____
_____

What I did today for myself is _____
_____
_____
_____

Date _____

Today I am thankful for _____
_____
_____
_____
_____

I realized today that _____
_____
_____

I felt happy today when _____
_____
_____
_____


Date _____

Today I am thankful for _____
_____
_____
_____
_____

I felt happy today when _____
_____
_____

What's going on well in my life is _____
_____
_____
_____

Date _____

Today I am thankful for _____
_____
_____
_____
_____

I relized today that _____ ___ ____
_____
_____
_____

I felt happy today when _____
_____
_____
_____

Date _____

Today I am thankful for _____
_____
_____
_____
_____

Good things I noticed today _____
_____
_____

What's going on well in my life is _____
_____
_____
_____

Date _____

Today I am thankful for _____
_____
_____
_____
_____

I realized today that _____
_____
_____

I felt happy today when _____
_____
_____
_____

Date _____

Today I am thankful for _____
_____
_____
_____
_____

I felt happy today when _____
_____
_____

What's going on well in my life is _____
_____
_____
_____

# Weekly Gratitude

This week I am grateful for _____

_____

_____

_____

_____

_____

_____

_____

_____


5 things I am lucky to have in my life _____

_____

_____

_____

_____

_____

_____

_____

_____


3 people I am lucky to have right now _____

_____

_____

_____

_____

_____

Date _____

Today I am thankful for _____
_____
_____
_____
_____

I am proud of myself because _____
_____
_____
_____
_____

My small victory today _____
_____


Date _____

Today I am thankful for _____
_____
_____
_____
_____

The person I am thankful for today is _____
_____
_____

What I did today for myself is _____
_____
_____
_____

Date _____

Today I am thankful for _____

_____

_____

_____

_____

I realized today that _____

_____

_____

I felt happy today when _____

_____

_____

_____

Date _____

Today I am thankful for _____

_____

_____

_____

_____

I felt happy today when _____

_____

_____

What's going on well in my life is _____

_____

_____

_____

Date _____

Today I am thankful for _____

_____

_____

_____

_____

I relized today that _____

_____

_____

_____

I felt happy today when _____

_____

_____

_____


Date _____

Today I am thankful for _____

_____

_____

_____

_____

Good things I noticed today _____

_____

_____

What's going on well in my life is _____

_____

_____

_____

Date _____

Today I am thankful for _____
_____
_____
_____
_____

I am proud of myself because _____
_____
_____
_____
_____

My small victory today _____
_____


Date _____

Today I am thankful for _____
_____
_____
_____
_____

The person I am thankful for today is _____
_____
_____

What I did today for myself is _____
_____
_____
_____

Date \_\_\_\_\_

Today I am thankful for _____
_____
_____
_____
_____

I realized today that _____
_____
_____

I felt happy today when _____
_____
_____
_____

Date \_\_\_\_\_

Today I am thankful for _____
_____
_____
_____
_____

I felt happy today when _____
_____
_____

What's going on well in my life is _____
_____
_____
_____

Date _____

Today I am thankful for _____
_____
_____
_____
_____

I relized today that _____
_____
_____
_____

I felt happy today when _____
_____
_____
_____

Date _____

Today I am thankful for _____
_____
_____
_____
_____

Good things I noticed today _____
_____
_____

What's going on well in my life is _____
_____
_____
_____

Date _____

Today I am thankful for _____
_____
_____
_____
_____

I realized today that _____
_____
_____

I felt happy today when _____
_____
_____
_____


Date _____

Today I am thankful for _____
_____
_____
_____
_____

I felt happy today when _____
_____
_____

What's going on well in my life is _____
_____
_____
_____

# Weekly Gratitude

This week I am grateful for _____

_____

_____

_____

_____

_____

_____

_____

_____

5 things I am lucky to have in my life _____

_____

_____

_____

_____

_____

_____

_____

_____

3 people I am lucky to have right now _____

_____

_____

_____

_____

Date _____

Today I am thankful for _____
_____
_____
_____
_____

I am proud of myself because _____
_____
_____
_____
_____

My small victory today _____
_____


Date _____

Today I am thankful for _____
_____
_____
_____
_____

The person I am thankful for today is _____
_____
_____

What I did today for myself is _____
_____
_____
_____

Date _____

Today I am thankful for _____
_____
_____
_____
_____

I realized today that _____
_____
_____

I felt happy today when _____
_____
_____
_____


Date _____

Today I am thankful for _____
_____
_____
_____
_____

I felt happy today when _____
_____
_____

What's going on well in my life is _____
_____
_____
_____

Date _____

Today I am thankful for _____

_____

_____

_____

_____

I relized today that _____

_____

_____

_____

I felt happy today when _____

_____

_____

_____

Date _____

Today I am thankful for _____

_____

_____

_____

_____

Good things I noticed today _____

_____

_____

What's going on well in my life is _____

_____

_____

_____

Date _____

Today I am thankful for _____
_____
_____
_____
_____

I am proud of myself because _____
_____
_____
_____
_____

My small victory today _____
_____


Date _____

Today I am thankful for _____
_____
_____
_____

The person I am thankful for today is _____
_____
_____

What I did today for myself is _____
_____
_____
_____

Date _____

Today I am thankful for _____
_____
_____
_____
_____

I realized today that _____
_____
_____

I felt happy today when _____
_____
_____
_____

Date _____

Today I am thankful for _____
_____
_____
_____
_____

I felt happy today when _____
_____
_____

What's going on well in my life is _____
_____
_____
_____

Date _____

Today I am thankful for _____

_____

_____

_____

_____

I relized today that _____

_____

_____

_____

I felt happy today when _____

_____

_____

_____

Date _____

Today I am thankful for _____

_____

_____

_____

_____

Good things I noticed today _____

_____

_____

What's going on well in my life is _____

_____

_____

_____

Date _____

Today I am thankful for _____

_____

_____

_____

_____

I realized today that _____

_____

_____

I felt happy today when _____

_____

_____

_____

Date _____

Today I am thankful for _____

_____

_____

_____

_____

I felt happy today when _____

_____

_____

What's going on well in my life is _____

_____

_____

_____

# Weekly Gratitude

This week I am grateful for _____

_____

_____

_____

_____

_____

_____

_____

_____


5 things I am lucky to have in my life _____

_____

_____

_____

_____

_____

_____

_____

_____


3 people I am lucky to have right now _____

_____

_____

_____

_____

Date _____

Today I am thankful for _____
_____
_____
_____
_____

I am proud of myself because _____
_____
_____
_____
_____

My small victory today _____
_____


Date _____

Today I am thankful for _____
_____
_____
_____
_____

The person I am thankful for today is _____
_____
_____

What I did today for myself is _____
_____
_____
_____

Date _____

Today I am thankful for _____
_____
_____
_____
_____

I realized today that _____
_____
_____

I felt happy today when _____
_____
_____
_____


Date _____

Today I am thankful for _____
_____
_____
_____
_____

I felt happy today when _____
_____
_____

What's going on well in my life is _____
_____
_____
_____

Date _____

Today I am thankful for _____
_____
_____
_____
_____

I relized today that _____
_____
_____
_____

I felt happy today when _____
_____
_____
_____

Date _____

Today I am thankful for _____
_____
_____
_____
_____

Good things I noticed today _____
_____
_____

What's going on well in my life is _____
_____
_____
_____

Date _____

Today I am thankful for _____
_____
_____
_____
_____

I am proud of myself because _____
_____
_____
_____
_____

My small victory today _____
_____


Date _____

Today I am thankful for _____
_____
_____
_____
_____

The person I am thankful for today is _____
_____
_____

What I did today for myself is _____
_____
_____
_____

Date _____

Today I am thankful for _____

_____

_____

_____

_____

I realized today that _____

_____

_____

I felt happy today when _____

_____

_____

_____


Date _____

Today I am thankful for _____

_____

_____

_____

_____

I felt happy today when _____

_____

_____

What's going on well in my life is _____

_____

_____

_____

Date _____

Today I am thankful for _____

_____

_____

_____

_____

I relized today that _____

_____

_____

_____

I felt happy today when _____

_____

_____

_____

Date _____

Today I am thankful for _____

_____

_____

_____

_____

Good things I noticed today _____

_____

_____

What's going on well in my life is _____

_____

_____

_____

Date _____

Today I am thankful for _____

_____

_____

_____

_____

I realized today that _____

_____

_____

I felt happy today when _____

_____

_____

_____


Date _____

Today I am thankful for _____

_____

_____

_____

_____

I felt happy today when _____

_____

_____

What's going on well in my life is _____

_____

_____

_____

# Weekly Gratitude

This week I am grateful for _____

_____

_____

_____

_____

_____

_____

_____

_____

5 things I am lucky to have in my life _____

_____

_____

_____

_____

_____

_____

_____

3 people I am lucky to have right now _____

_____

_____

_____

_____

Date _____

Today I am thankful for _____
_____
_____
_____
_____

I am proud of myself because _____
_____
_____
_____
_____

My small victory today _____
_____

Date _____

Today I am thankful for _____
_____
_____
_____
_____

The person I am thankful for today is _____
_____
_____

What I did today for myself is _____
_____
_____
_____

Date _____

Today I am thankful for _____
_____
_____
_____
_____

I realized today that _____
_____
_____

I felt happy today when _____
_____
_____
_____


Date _____

Today I am thankful for _____
_____
_____
_____
_____

I felt happy today when _____
_____
_____

What's going on well in my life is _____
_____
_____
_____

Date _____

Today I am thankful for _____
_____
_____
_____
_____

I relized today that _____
_____
_____
_____

I felt happy today when _____
_____
_____
_____

Date _____

Today I am thankful for _____
_____
_____
_____
_____

Good things I noticed today _____
_____
_____

What's going on well in my life is _____
_____
_____
_____

Date _____

Today I am thankful for _____
_____
_____
_____
_____

I am proud of myself because _____
_____
_____
_____
_____

My small victory today _____
_____

Date _____

Today I am thankful for _____
_____
_____
_____
_____

The person I am thankful for today is _____
_____
_____

What I did today for myself is _____
_____
_____
_____

Date _____

Today I am thankful for _____
_____
_____
_____
_____

I realized today that _____
_____
_____

I felt happy today when _____
_____
_____
_____

Date _____

Today I am thankful for _____
_____
_____
_____
_____

I felt happy today when _____
_____
_____

What's going on well in my life is _____
_____
_____
_____

Date _____

Today I am thankful for _____

_____

_____

_____

_____

I relized today that _____

_____

_____

_____

I felt happy today when _____

_____

_____

_____


Date _____

Today I am thankful for _____

_____

_____

_____

_____

Good things I noticed today _____

_____

_____

What's going on well in my life is _____

_____

_____

_____

Date _____

Today I am thankful for _____
_____
_____
_____
_____

I realized today that _____
_____
_____

I felt happy today when _____
_____
_____
_____

Date _____

Today I am thankful for _____
_____
_____
_____
_____

I felt happy today when _____
_____
_____

What's going on well in my life is _____
_____
_____
_____

# Weekly Gratitude

This week I am grateful for _____

_____

_____

_____

_____

_____

_____

_____

5 things I am lucky to have in my life _____

_____

_____

_____

_____

_____

_____

_____

_____

3 people I am lucky to have right now _____

_____

_____

_____

_____

Date _____

Today I am thankful for _____
_____
_____
_____
_____

I am proud of myself because _____
_____
_____
_____
_____

My small victory today _____
_____

Date _____

Today I am thankful for _____
_____
_____
_____
_____

The person I am thankful for today is _____
_____
_____

What I did today for myself is _____
_____
_____
_____

Date _____

Today I am thankful for _____
_____
_____
_____
_____

I realized today that _____
_____
_____

I felt happy today when _____
_____
_____
_____


Date _____

Today I am thankful for _____
_____
_____
_____
_____

I felt happy today when _____
_____
_____

What's going on well in my life is _____
_____
_____
_____

Date _____

Today I am thankful for _____
_____
_____
_____
_____

I relized today that _____
_____
_____
_____

I felt happy today when _____
_____
_____
_____

Date _____

Today I am thankful for _____
_____
_____
_____
_____

Good things I noticed today _____
_____
_____

What's going on well in my life is _____
_____
_____
_____

Date \_\_\_\_\_

Today I am thankful for _____
_____
_____
_____
_____

I am proud of myself because _____
_____
_____
_____
_____

My small victory today _____
_____

Date \_\_\_\_\_

Today I am thankful for _____
_____
_____
_____
_____

The person I am thankful for today is _____
_____
_____

What I did today for myself is _____
_____
_____
_____

Date _____

Today I am thankful for _____
_____
_____
_____
_____

I realized today that _____
_____
_____

I felt happy today when _____
_____
_____
_____

Date _____

Today I am thankful for _____
_____
_____
_____
_____

I felt happy today when _____
_____
_____

What's going on well in my life is _____
_____
_____
_____

Date _____

Today I am thankful for _____
_____
_____
_____
_____

I relized today that _____
_____
_____
_____

I felt happy today when _____
_____
_____
_____

Date _____

Today I am thankful for _____
_____
_____
_____
_____

Good things I noticed today _____
_____
_____

What's going on well in my life is _____
_____
_____
_____

Date _____

Today I am thankful for _____
_____
_____
_____
_____

I realized today that _____
_____
_____

I felt happy today when _____
_____
_____
_____

Date _____

Today I am thankful for _____
_____
_____
_____
_____

I felt happy today when _____
_____
_____

What's going on well in my life is _____
_____
_____
_____

# Weekly Gratitude

This week I am grateful for _____

_____

_____

_____

_____

_____

_____

_____

_____


5 things I am lucky to have in my life _____

_____

_____

_____

_____

_____

_____

_____

_____

_____


3 people I am lucky to have right now _____

_____

_____

_____

_____

Date _____

Today I am thankful for _____
_____
_____
_____
_____

I am proud of myself because _____
_____
_____
_____
_____

My small victory today _____
_____


Date _____

Today I am thankful for _____
_____
_____
_____
_____

The person I am thankful for today is _____
_____
_____

What I did today for myself is _____
_____
_____
_____

Date _____

Today I am thankful for _____

_____

_____

_____

_____

I realized today that _____

_____

_____

I felt happy today when _____

_____

_____

_____


Date _____

Today I am thankful for _____

_____

_____

_____

_____

I felt happy today when _____

_____

_____

What's going on well in my life is _____

_____

_____

_____

Date _____

Today I am thankful for _____
_____
_____
_____
_____

I relized today that _____
_____
_____
_____

I felt happy today when _____
_____
_____
_____

Date _____

Today I am thankful for _____
_____
_____
_____
_____

Good things I noticed today _____
_____
_____

What's going on well in my life is _____
_____
_____
_____

Date _____

Today I am thankful for _____
_____
_____
_____
_____

I am proud of myself because _____
_____
_____
_____
_____

My small victory today _____
_____

Date _____

Today I am thankful for _____
_____
_____
_____
_____

The person I am thankful for today is _____
_____
_____

What I did today for myself is _____
_____
_____
_____

Date _____

Today I am thankful for _____

_____

_____

_____

_____

I realized today that _____

_____

_____

I felt happy today when _____

_____

_____

_____


Date _____

Today I am thankful for _____

_____

_____

_____

_____

I felt happy today when _____

_____

_____

What's going on well in my life is _____

_____

_____

_____

Date _____

Today I am thankful for _____
_____
_____
_____
_____

I relized today that _____
_____
_____
_____

I felt happy today when _____
_____
_____
_____

Date _____

Today I am thankful for _____
_____
_____
_____
_____

Good things I noticed today _____
_____
_____

What's going on well in my life is _____
_____
_____
_____

Date _____

Today I am thankful for _____

_____

_____

_____

_____

I realized today that _____

_____

_____

I felt happy today when _____

_____

_____

_____

Date _____

Today I am thankful for _____

_____

_____

_____

_____

I felt happy today when _____

_____

_____

What's going on well in my life is _____

_____

_____

_____

# Weekly Gratitude

This week I am grateful for _____

_____

_____

_____

_____

_____

_____

_____

_____

5 things I am lucky to have in my life _____

_____

_____

_____

_____

_____

_____

_____

3 people I am lucky to have right now _____

_____

_____

_____

_____

Date _____

Today I am thankful for _____

_____

_____

_____

_____

I am proud of myself because _____

_____

_____

_____

_____

My small victory today _____

_____


Date _____

Today I am thankful for _____

_____

_____

_____

_____

The person I am thankful for today is _____

_____

_____

What I did today for myself is _____

_____

_____

_____

Date _____

Today I am thankful for _____

_____

_____

_____

_____

I realized today that _____

_____

_____

I felt happy today when _____

_____

_____

_____

Date _____

Today I am thankful for _____

_____

_____

_____

_____

I felt happy today when _____

_____

_____

What's going on well in my life is _____

_____

_____

_____

Date _____

Today I am thankful for _____
_____
_____
_____
_____

I relized today that _____
_____
_____
_____

I felt happy today when _____
_____
_____
_____

Date _____

Today I am thankful for _____
_____
_____
_____
_____

Good things I noticed today _____
_____
_____

What's going on well in my life is _____
_____
_____
_____

Date _____

Today I am thankful for _____
_____
_____
_____
_____

I am proud of myself because _____
_____
_____
_____
_____

My small victory today _____
_____


Date _____

Today I am thankful for _____
_____
_____
_____
_____

The person I am thankful for today is _____
_____
_____

What I did today for myself is _____
_____
_____
_____

Date _____

Today I am thankful for _____

_____

_____

_____

_____

_____

I realized today that _____

_____

_____

I felt happy today when _____

_____

_____

_____


Date _____

Today I am thankful for _____

_____

_____

_____

_____

_____

I felt happy today when _____

_____

_____

What's going on well in my life is _____

_____

_____

_____

Date _____

Today I am thankful for _____
_____
_____
_____
_____

I relized today that _____
_____
_____
_____

I felt happy today when _____
_____
_____
_____

Date _____

Today I am thankful for _____
_____
_____
_____
_____

Good things I noticed today _____
_____
_____

What's going on well in my life is _____
_____
_____
_____

Date _____

Today I am thankful for _____
_____
_____
_____
_____
_____

I realized today that _____
_____
_____

I felt happy today when _____
_____
_____
_____

Date _____

Today I am thankful for _____
_____
_____
_____
_____
_____

I felt happy today when _____
_____
_____

What's going on well in my life is _____
_____
_____
_____

# Weekly Gratitude

This week I am grateful for _____

_____

_____

_____

_____

_____

_____

_____

_____


5 things I am lucky to have in my life _____

_____

_____

_____

_____

_____

_____


3 people I am lucky to have right now _____

_____

_____

_____

_____

Date _____

Today I am thankful for _____

_____

_____

_____

_____

I am proud of myself because _____

_____

_____

_____

_____

My small victory today _____

_____


Date _____

Today I am thankful for _____

_____

_____

_____

_____

The person I am thankful for today is _____

_____

_____

What I did today for myself is _____

_____

_____

_____

Date _____

Today I am thankful for _____
_____
_____
_____
_____

I realized today that _____
_____
_____

I felt happy today when _____
_____
_____
_____

Date _____

Today I am thankful for _____
_____
_____
_____
_____

I felt happy today when _____
_____
_____

What's going on well in my life is _____
_____
_____
_____

Date _____

Today I am thankful for _____
_____
_____
_____
_____

I relized today that _____
_____
_____
_____

I felt happy today when _____
_____
_____
_____

Date _____

Today I am thankful for _____
_____
_____
_____
_____

Good things I noticed today _____
_____
_____

What's going on well in my life is _____
_____
_____
_____

Date _____

Today I am thankful for _____
_____
_____
_____
_____

I am proud of myself because _____
_____
_____
_____
_____

My small victory today _____
_____

Date _____

Today I am thankful for _____
_____
_____
_____
_____

The person I am thankful for today is _____
_____
_____

What I did today for myself is _____
_____
_____
_____

Date _____

Today I am thankful for _____

_____

_____

_____

_____

I realized today that _____

_____

_____

I felt happy today when _____

_____

_____

_____


Date _____

Today I am thankful for _____

_____

_____

_____

_____

I felt happy today when _____

_____

_____

What's going on well in my life is _____

_____

_____

_____

Date \_\_\_\_\_

Today I am thankful for _____
_____
_____
_____
_____

I relized today that _____
_____
_____
_____

I felt happy today when _____
_____
_____
_____

Date \_\_\_\_\_

Today I am thankful for _____
_____
_____
_____
_____

Good things I noticed today _____
_____
_____

What's going on well in my life is _____
_____
_____
_____

Date _____

Today I am thankful for _____
_____
_____
_____
_____

I realized today that _____
_____
_____

I felt happy today when _____
_____
_____
_____

Date _____

Today I am thankful for _____
_____
_____
_____
_____

I felt happy today when _____
_____
_____

What's going on well in my life is _____
_____
_____
_____

# Weekly Gratitude

This week I am grateful for _____

_____

_____

_____

_____

_____

_____

_____

_____

_____


5 things I am lucky to have in my life _____

_____

_____

_____

_____

_____

_____

_____

_____


3 people I am lucky to have right now _____

_____

_____

_____

_____

Date _____

Today I am thankful for _____
_____
_____
_____
_____

I am proud of myself because _____
_____
_____
_____
_____

My small victory today _____
_____

Date _____

Today I am thankful for _____
_____
_____
_____
_____

The person I am thankful for today is _____
_____
_____

What I did today for myself is _____
_____
_____
_____

Date _____

Today I am thankful for _____
_____
_____
_____
_____

I realized today that _____
_____
_____

I felt happy today when _____
_____
_____
_____


Date _____

Today I am thankful for _____
_____
_____
_____
_____

I felt happy today when _____
_____
_____

What's going on well in my life is _____
_____
_____
_____

Date \_\_\_\_\_

Today I am thankful for _____
_____
_____
_____
_____

I relized today that _____
_____
_____
_____

I felt happy today when _____
_____
_____
_____

Date \_\_\_\_\_

Today I am thankful for _____
_____
_____
_____
_____

Good things I noticed today _____
_____
_____

What's going on well in my life is _____
_____
_____
_____

Date _____

Today I am thankful for _____

_____

_____

_____

_____

I am proud of myself because _____

_____

_____

_____

_____

My small victory today _____

_____


Date _____

Today I am thankful for _____

_____

_____

_____

_____

The person I am thankful for today is _____

_____

_____

What I did today for myself is _____

_____

_____

_____

Date _____

Today I am thankful for _____
_____
_____
_____
_____

I realized today that _____
_____
_____

I felt happy today when _____
_____
_____
_____


Date _____

Today I am thankful for _____
_____
_____
_____
_____

I felt happy today when _____
_____
_____

What's going on well in my life is _____
_____
_____
_____

Date _____

Today I am thankful for _____
_____
_____
_____
_____

I relized today that _____
_____
_____
_____

I felt happy today when _____
_____
_____
_____


Date _____

Today I am thankful for _____
_____
_____
_____
_____

Good things I noticed today _____
_____
_____

What's going on well in my life is _____
_____
_____
_____

Date _____

Today I am thankful for _____
_____
_____
_____
_____

I realized today that _____
_____
_____

I felt happy today when _____
_____
_____
_____


Date _____

Today I am thankful for _____
_____
_____
_____
_____

I felt happy today when _____
_____
_____

What's going on well in my life is _____
_____
_____
_____

# Weekly Gratitude

This week I am grateful for _____

_____

_____

_____

_____

_____

_____

_____

_____

5 things I am lucky to have in my life _____

_____

_____

_____

_____

_____

_____

_____

3 people I am lucky to have right now _____

_____

_____

_____

_____

My thoughts _____

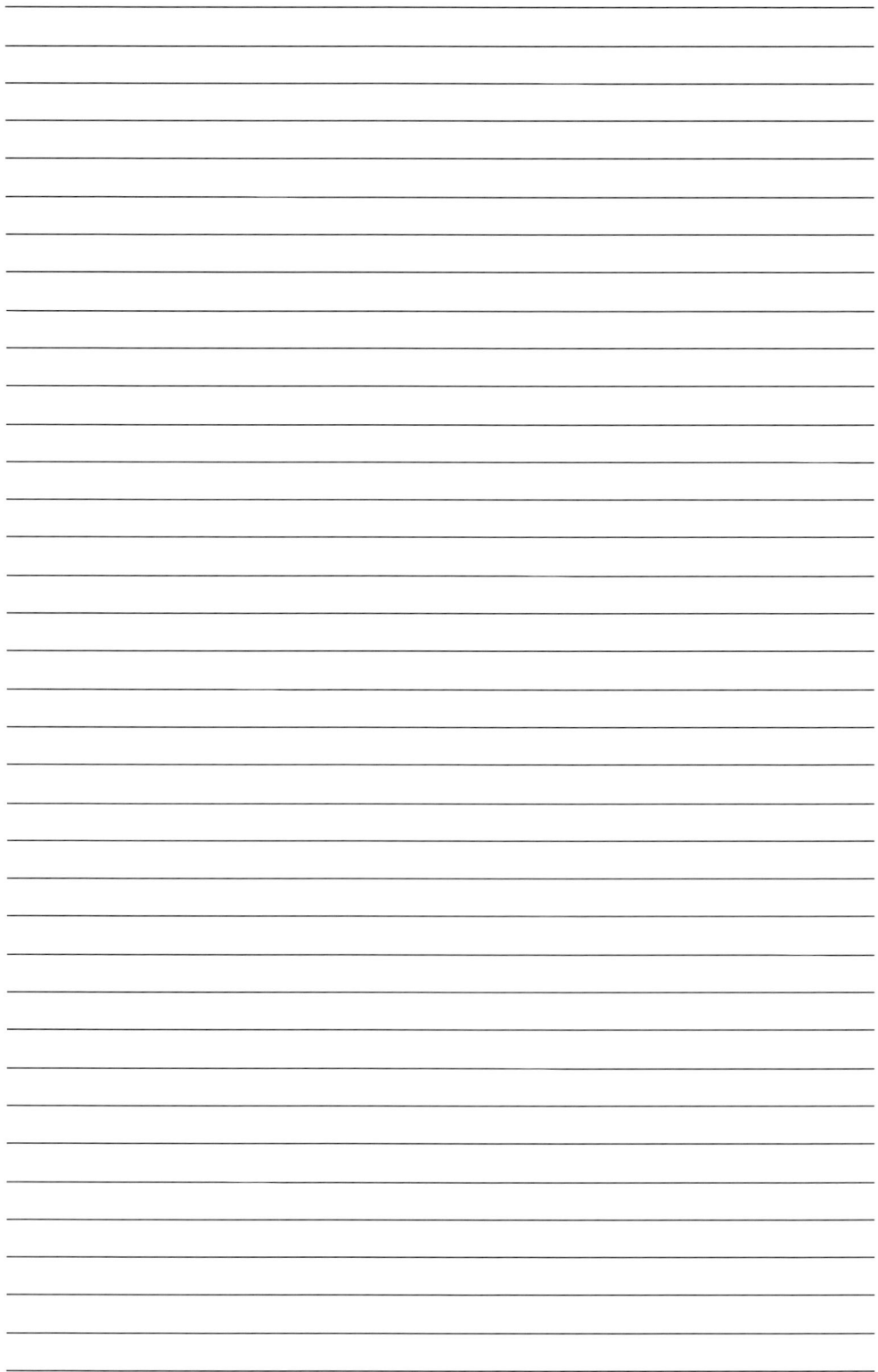

# Disclaimer

This book contains opinions and ideas of the author and is meant to teach the reader informative and helpful knowledge while due care should be taken by the user in the application of the information provided. The instructions and strategies are possibly not right for every reader and there is no guarantee that they work for everyone. Using this book and implementing the information therein contained is explicitly your own responsibility and risk. This work with all its contents, does not guarantee correctness, completion, quality or correctness of the provided information. Misinformation or misprints cannot be completely eliminated. Human mistake is real!

Printed in Great Britain
by Amazon